Did You Hear the News?

Sanya Whittaker Gragg, MSW
illustrated by Kim Holt

Email: Memorizethe5@gmail.com
Website: www.sanyagragg.com
Twitter: @memorizethe5
Instagram: @memorizethe5

ISBN: 978-1-7365353-0-1

Illustrations by Kim Holt

Book design by Sarah E. Holroyd (https://sleepingcatbooks.com)

Dedicated to the brown guys in my life: Derrick, Avery & Phillip-Raymond...I pray each time you walk out the door.
—SWG

Momma, did you hear the news?
Another man was shot.
They say he had a little girl,
Bet she misses him a lot.

Yes, my son, I heard the news.
I prayed for them today.
But now I just don't have the words,
I don't know what to say.

I really just don't understand.
I thought cops were good guys.
But every day I watch tv,
They're taking someone's life.

One boy was eating skittles.
Dad, I like to eat them too!
Another played his music loud,
Just like I sometimes do.

I wish I had an answer, son
To calm your fears today.
I think it's time we have "THE TALK"
Come have a seat, OK?

I know you boys are youngsters,
But life goes fast you see.
I want to share this with you,
Words your Granny shared with me.

A to the
L to the
I-V-E
Come home ALIVE
That is the key!

I'm sure this may sound scary,
And hard to understand.
But boys you have to promise,
You will do as I command.

If ever you are driving,
And see those flashing lights;
These things you must remember
To come home safe, alright?

We're not old enough to drive.
Do we have to know this now?
I'll repeat these words often my sons,
As much as time allows.

A to the
L to the
I-V-E
Come home ALIVE
That is the key!

Each letter stands for something.
Repeat them in your head.
So if you get pulled over,
You'll remember what we've said.

ALWAYS USE YOUR MANNERS

ALWAYS USE YOUR MANNERS!
Yes sir. No sir. Be polite.
NO attitude. And <u>never</u> talk back.
Be respectful. Day and night.

LISTEN AND COMPLY

LISTEN AND COMPLY!
Do exactly as they say.
Do not debate or argue.
Or your life you just might pay!

IN CONTROL

STAY CALM

STAY COOL

Stay IN CONTROL of your emotions!
Even if you are upset.
Speak low and slow. Watch your tone.
Or they'll see you as a threat.

VISIBLE HANDS ALWAYS

VISIBLE hands at ALL times!
Like a clock. On 10 and 2.
This may be the most important,
So please be sure you do!

EXPLAIN ANY MOVEMENT

EXPLAIN any movement!
"Sir, may I get my wallet please?"
NO SUDDEN MOVEMENTS EVER!
Don't reach. Don't grab. Don't sneeze!

I know this is a lot my sons.
I know you're both just kids.
But these things you must remember.
These rules you can't forget.

One boy was holding his toy gun.
He was playing in the park!
I'm mad and scared to walk our dog.
Especially when it's dark!

What about the policemen, Mom?
Thought they were all good guys.
If they don't like us "cause we're black",
What matters? Not our lives!

You have a right to be mad and sad
With all that's going on.
But ALL policemen are not bad.
You're wrong son. You ARE WRONG!

They have families just like us.
They're Moms and Daddies too.
They want to get home safe at night.
We pray for those in blue!

The mean ones are the reason why
We had this talk today.
So if you do get stopped by one,
You'll know just what to say.

#NOMORE

We love you both so much, our sons
And this you know is true.
Your name can't be a hashtag!!
Bet those mommas said that too.

So make sure all your friends know
To Memorize the FIVE!
These words can make a difference
So you all come home ALIVE!

A to the L to the I-V-E

Come home

ALIVE

THAT IS THE KEY!

MEMORIZE THE 5

A ALWAYS USE YOUR MANNERS

L LISTEN AND COMPLY

I IN CONTROL OF EMOTIONS

V VISIBLE HANDS ALWAYS

E EXPLAIN ANY MOVEMENT

CPSIA information can be obtained
at www.ICGtesting.com
Printed in the USA
LVHW071530180222
711484LV00012B/738

9 781736 535301